Contents

D1784887

Introduction

The activities in this book provide ongoing practice of key skills in Number, Shape and Measures. They are short, snappy, fun activities which may be used in the following contexts:

- between lessons
- before play
- before going home
- before assembly
- first thing in the morning
- during PE
- during informal 'on the rug' sessions
- after more formal written mathematics
- before introducing the next mathematical topic
- as revision and rehearsal.

The idea behind this book is that the activities provide a means of keeping a mathematical concept, skill or operation 'on-the-go' (i.e. simmering) and alive in the children's minds. In order to become numerate adults, children need to develop and refine their mental techniques with numbers. These simmering activities allow children to practise their strategies in the context of a game or other fun activity.

It is clear that a major factor in helping children to develop a real mental facility with numbers is the presence of regular activities. The golden rule is 'little and often'. Children will enjoy a quick game played on the rug or while they are waiting to go into the hall for assembly. Some games become real favourites and children will ask to play them repeatedly.

The simmering activities are categorised under topic headings for easy access. Some games are playable at a variety of levels (with the teacher varying the numbers as appropriate). Many of the activities are readily adaptable to a slightly different context. All the activities are related to the relevant Teacher Cards and units of work in Abacus.

Section 1: Counting and writing numbers

1.1 Numbers to 1000

Abacus 5
N1

- Ask one child for a 3-digit starting number, e.g. 345. Count on in unison: 345, 346, 347, ... Repeat, asking individual children, in turn, to say the next number. If a child says a multiple of ten, they stand up. If on their next turn they say an even number, they sit down.

- Write a 3-digit starting number on the board, e.g. 287. Place the children in pairs. Ask each pair, in turn, to count on in tens and write the next number, e.g. 297, 307, 317, ... If a pair says or writes the wrong number, the class shout out the correct answer.

1.2 Numbers to 10 000

Abacus 5
N1

- Choose a 4-digit starting number and write it on the board, e.g. 2349. Divide the class in two teams. Point to a child in one team, who must say the number one hundred more, i.e. 2449. Write it on the board. If correct, that team scores ten points. Continue, choosing different children in each team, checking the answer and awarding points.

- Write 10 000 on the board. Place the children in pairs. Count back in tens, by asking different pairs to write the next number: 9990, 9980, 9970, ... The pairs should be ready when it is their turn. Count along the line of numbers in unison.

1.3   Numbers over 10 000

Abacus 5
N1

- Write a 5-digit starting number on the board, e.g. 23 418. Tell the class they are counting in ones, tens or hundreds. Ask five children, in turn, to come to the front and write the next number on a piece of paper (hidden from the rest of the class). Ask another child to read the five numbers aloud in order. Are they correct? Chant them in unison.

  Repeat.

- Write five 5-digit numbers on the board, e.g. 31 956, 72 399, 96 544, 12 121, 62 871. Choose a child to add one hundred to one of the numbers and say the answer aloud. The others say which number they started with.

  Repeat with different children for adding ten, or for adding one thousand.

  When the children are confident they can decide themselves how much to add.

1.4   Decimal numbers (tenths)

Abacus 5   **Abacus 6**
N21   N1, N22

- **Decimal number line (1·0, 1·1, ... 2)**
  Point to a number and start the children counting forwards along the line: *one point three, one point four, ... one point eight.* Clap your hands, and the children must immediately start counting backwards: *one point seven, one point six, ...*

- **A dice**
  Write a decimal target number on the board, e.g. 4·2.

  Throw the dice twice and make a decimal number, e.g. 2·3. Count from the dice number to the target number (decide whether to count forwards or backwards).

  Count in unison or around the class, pointing to each child in turn who says the next number. When the target is reached, that child throws the dice to create the next starting number.

1.5   Decimal numbers (hundredths)

Abacus 5
N21

Abacus 6
N1, N22

- Count round the class in hundredths starting at a number between 0 and 1, e.g. 0·32: *zero point three two, zero point three three, zero point three four, zero point three five, ...* Occasionally stop and ask a child to write their number on the board. Focus particularly on number which cross the tenth's decade (e.g. 0·39, 0·40).

- Divide the class into four teams. Give each team a piece of paper. Write four starting numbers on the board and allocate one to each team. Within a team the children take turns to count on in hundredths from their starting number, writing the numbers. When each child has written a number, the teams chant down their list in unison. Award points for correctness, and chanting.

1.6   Negative numbers

Abacus 5
N30

Abacus 6
N29, N30

- Draw a lift on the board and write a 'floor', e.g. 7. Ask a child a question, e.g. *I want to go down 10 floors. Where will I get out?* Write 'down 10 floors' on the board. That child writes the answer and, if correct, asks another child a question, starting from the last floor.

Section 2: Ordering numbers

2.1   Numbers to 1000

Abacus 5
N1

● Give each child a piece of paper. They each write a 3-digit number. Write a 3-digit number on the board, e.g. 500. Choose a child to write their number on the board next to yours. Is it larger or smaller? Draw the appropriate sign (< or >) between the two.

Repeat, asking a child to draw the correct sign.

2.2   Numbers to 10 000

Abacus 5
N1

● Choose four children to each write a 4-digit number on the board at the same time. Consult the class. Which number is largest? Write this on a piece of paper. Choose a child to hold it. Which number is next largest? Write this number on another piece of paper and choose a child to hold it, standing next to the first child. Continue until the four children are standing in a line with numbers from largest to smallest.

Repeat.

● Place the children in pairs. Each pair writes a 4-digit number on a piece of paper. Give a range of numbers and write it on the board, e.g. between 2000 and 3000. All the pairs with numbers in this range must stand up. Check their numbers.

Repeat for a different range, e.g. between 6000 and 7000.

2.3 Numbers over 10 000

Abacus 5
N1

- Draw a number line with ten divisions on the board. Number it 12 000, 12 100, 12 200, ... 13 000.

  Choose three children to leave the room. Ask the remainder to choose a number within the range, e.g. 12 359. Write it on the board and ask the children to copy it. Rub it off the board and invite the three children back in.

  They have six questions to help them guess the chosen number, e.g. *Is it less than 12 500? Is it between 12 300 and 12 400?*

  Repeat.

- Write a starting number on the board, e.g. 13 506. Read it aloud. Choose a child and ask them to say a number that is over 100 more. They write the number on the board, and ask another child a question, e.g. say a number that is over 1000 less than this number.

  Continue, encouraging the children to be inventive with their questions.

2.4 Decimal numbers (tenths)

Abacus 5
N21

Abacus 6
N2

- Write a range of numbers on the board, e.g. between 0·1 and 5·0. Choose three children to write a number within this range on a piece of paper, hidden from the class. The class ask questions to help them guess the number, each one 'costing' them 10p. Keep a record of how much they have spent. How much before they guess the number?

- Write an inequality sign on the board, e.g. >. Divide the class into two teams. Choose a child from Team A to write a decimal number with tenths on one side of the inequality sign, e.g. 2·3 >. They choose a child from Team B to write a correct second number in place. If correct, Team B scores a point.

  Repeat, with the teams taking turns to write the first number.

2.5   Decimal numbers (hundredths)

Abacus 5
N21

Abacus 6
N22

- Give each child a piece of paper. Ask each to write a decimal number with hundredths between 0 and 5 on their paper. Give a range, e.g. between 3·00 and 4·00, and ask children with a number in this range to write their number on the board.

  Discuss with the class which number is largest, next largest, ... Arrange the children in order, holding their numbers.

  Repeat for a different range.

- **A coin**
  Write a starting number on the board, e.g. 4·06. Choose a child to spin the coin. If it lands heads they say a number that is larger than the written number. If it lands tails they say a number that is smaller. Write their number on the board. That child then gives the coin to another to spin.

2.6   Negative numbers

Abacus 5
N30

Abacus 6
N29, N30

- **A dice, a coin**
  Write a negative number on the board, e.g. ⁻3. Choose two children, one to throw the dice and the other to spin the coin. If the coin lands heads the dice number is positive. If it lands tails the dice number is negative. The children add the dice throw to the starting number and say the answer. Write it on the board and ask the class to check. Repeat for different pairs.

Section 3: Place-value and rounding

3.1   Numbers up to 1000

Abacus 5
N1

- Draw a large place-value chart (H, T, U) on the board.

H	T	U

Choose a child to say a number, and write it on the chart, e.g. 506. Choose a second child to change just one digit (mentally) and say the new number aloud, e.g. *five hundred and twenty-six*. The other children say which digit has been changed (hundreds, tens or units).

Write the new number on the chart and repeat with a different child.

3.2   Numbers over 1000

Abacus 5
N1

- Choose a child to say a number between 1 and 100, e.g. 34. This is the number of thousands – write it on the board: 34 000. Choose another child to say a number between 0 and 9: the number of hundreds, e.g. 9. Choose a third child to say a number of tens, e.g. 5, and a fourth to say a number of units, e.g. 7.

Ask the class to write the full number. Check their answers and write it on the board: 34 957.

Repeat.

3.3   Decimal numbers

Abacus 5
N21

Abacus 6
N1, N22

- **Two sets of number cards (0 to 9)**
  Place the children in four teams. Draw two place-value charts (U, t, h) on the board.

U	t	h
	•	

  Shuffle the cards and deal one to each team. They discuss where to place their number in their chart. They are trying to make a large number. Once they have placed a number, they cannot move it.

  Repeat twice so that each team has a decimal number. The largest wins.

  Repeat, so that the smallest number wins.

3.4   Rounding to the nearest ten

Abacus 5
N2

Abacus 6
N1

- Choose a child and say a 2- or 3-digit number, e.g. 375. They round it to the nearest ten, i.e. 380. If correct, that child chooses another and says a number, e.g. 251. The second child rounds it to the nearest ten. Continue around the class, boys choosing girls, and girls choosing boys.

- Write ten 2- and 3- digit numbers on the board. Choose a child to round a number to the nearest ten (not revealing which number they have chosen), saying the answer aloud. The others must guess which number they chose. The first child then chooses another child to round a different number.

3.5 Rounding to the nearest hundred

Abacus 5
N2

Abacus 6
N1

- **A dice, cubes**

  Place the children in pairs and ask each pair to write a 3-digit number. Throw the dice and write that many hundreds on the board, e.g. 400. Any pair whose number rounds to this takes a cube, and writes a new number.

  Continue until one pair collects five cubes.

3.6 Rounding to the nearest thousand

Abacus 5
N2

Abacus 6
N1

- Write a number of thousands on the board, e.g. 13 000. Choose a child to say a number that has that number as its nearest thousand e.g. *twelve thousand, six hundred and ninety-nine*. They write it on the board. Discuss with the class to check it is correct. That child then chooses another to say a new number.

  After three or four children, write a new target number.

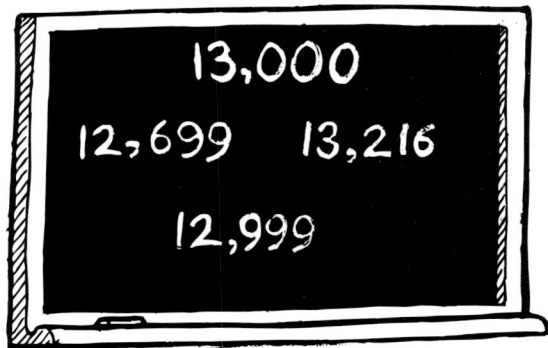

- Choose a child and say a 4- or 5-digit number, e.g. 24 587. They round it to the nearest thousand and say the answer, i.e. 25 000. If correct, that child chooses another and says a new number. Boys should choose girls and girls should choose boys. Encourage the children to choose a number that will challenge the next child.

3.7 Rounding decimals to the nearest whole number

Abacus 5
N35

Abacus 6
N1

- Write ten decimal numbers on the board (some with tenths, some with hundredths and some with both), e.g. 1·5, 10·6, 2·3, 4·7, 1·25, 2·33, 4·07, 9·12, 6·45, 6·54. Choose a child, who rounds a number to the nearest whole number (not saying which they have chosen), and says the answer aloud. The others guess which number they chose. If correct, that child chooses another child to round a different number. Continue until all the numbers have been rounded.

- **Two sets of number cards (0 to 9)**
  Write a target number on the board, e.g. 3. Divide the class into four teams. Shuffle the cards, and allow each team to pick three.

  Each team tries to arrange the cards to make a 2-place decimal number that rounds to the target.

  Any team which is correct is awarded ten points. Any team which is close (e.g. makes a number that rounds to 2 or 4) is awarded five points.

  Repeat.

3.8 Rounding decimals to the nearest tenth

Abacus 6
N1

- Place the children in pairs. Each pair writes a decimal number with tenths and hundredths. Choose a pair to round their number to the nearest tenth and write the answer on the board. The others guess which was their starting number. Write it on the board. Are they correct?

  Repeat for different pairs.

- Choose a child and say 2-place decimal number to them, e.g. 4·59. They have to come and write that number on the board. Then they have to round that number to the nearest tenth, e.g. 4·6. If they are correct, they choose a child (boys must choose girls and vice versa) and say a new 2-place decimal number to that child, e.g. 1·99. That child must write the number on the board and then round it to the nearest tenth and say the answer, e.g. 2·0. If they are correct, they choose a child and so on...

Section 4: Fractions

4.1   Simple fractions

Abacus 5
N7, N9

Abacus 6
N7

- Write on the board: 24, 100, 36, 72, 48, 12. Place the children in pairs. Each pair writes $\frac{1}{2}$ or $\frac{1}{4}$ or $\frac{1}{3}$ on a piece of paper. Choose a pair and point at one of the numbers. They calculate what their fraction of that number is. If they are correct they choose the next pair.

- **Number grid (1 to 100)**
  Choose a child and point to a number on the grid. They say what half of that number is. If correct that child chooses another and gives a number to halve (ensure it is even).

  Continue around the class.

4.2   Multiples of fractions

Abacus 5
N7, N9

Abacus 6
N7

- Write on the board: $\frac{3}{4}$, $\frac{2}{3}$, $\frac{5}{6}$ and $\frac{3}{5}$. Divide the class into four teams.

  Ask Team A: *If one quarter of the money in my purse is 12p, how much is three quarters?*

  If they answer correctly, they score a point.

  Ask Team B: *How much is in my purse?* If they answer correctly they score two points.

  Ask Team C: *If one fifth of the money in my purse is 10p, how much is three fifths?*

  Award a point for a correct answer.

  Ask Team D: *How much is in my purse?* Award two points for a correct answer.

  Continue around the class asking similar questions of each team.

4.3 Equivalent fractions

Abacus 5
N8, N22

Abacus 6
N8, N36

- Choose a child and say a starting fraction, e.g. *one half*. Write it on the board. They say an equivalent fraction, e.g. $\frac{3}{6}$. Write it on the board. If correct, that child chooses another to say a different equivalent fraction, e.g. $\frac{4}{8}$.

  Continue around the class.

  Repeat for a different starting fraction.

- **Multiplication square (1 to 100)**
  Say a starting fraction, e.g. $\frac{5}{8}$. Ask a child to point to two matching numbers on the grid in the same column. Choose different children to use the grid to generate equivalent fractions. How many can they make? Can they make equivalent fractions that don't appear on the grid?

4.4 Percentages

Abacus 5
N37

Abacus 6
N35

- Draw some items on the board, e.g. football shirts, tapes, videos, ... Give each one a price which is a multiple of ten, e.g. shirt: £30.

  Ask different children to calculate 10% of an item. Ask others to calculate 20% of an item.

  Continue asking different children to calculate percentages of particular items.

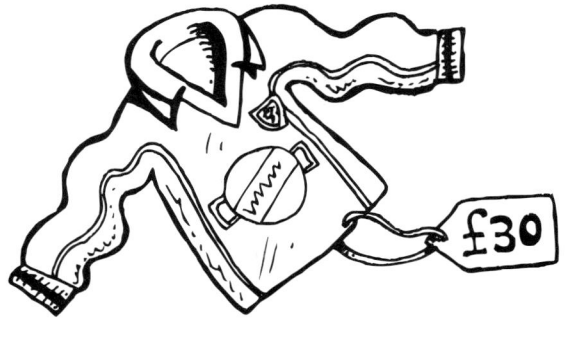

Section 5: Addition

5.1   Addition bonds

Abacus 5
N10, N36, N38

- Choose a child and 'throw' them a number, e.g. 30. They respond immediately with the number that makes 100, i.e. 70. They choose another child and throw them a new number. Continue around the class.

  Each child has three chances to make a mistake or hesitate.

  Variation Play with numbers that add to make 10 or 20.

  Variation Play with numbers which add to make 100, but restrict the children to multiples of five.

5.2   Adding 10 or multiples of 10

Abacus 5
N11

- Choose a child and say a 2- or 3-digit number, e.g. 234. They add ten and say the answer, i.e. 244. If correct, that child chooses another and says a number. The second child adds ten and says the answer. Continue around the class.

  Each child has three chances to make a mistake or hesitate.

- **A dice**
  Write on the board: 176, 58, 361, 94, 127, 88, 35.

  Divide the class into two teams. Choose a child to throw the dice and then add that number of tens to one of the numbers on the board. They shouldn't reveal which number they chose, but say the answer aloud. Their team guesses which number they chose, and scores a point for a correct answer.

  Continue, choosing different children from each team to throw the dice.

One hundred and twenty four.

5.3   Adding near multiples of ten
Abacus 5   **Abacus 6**
N24   N11

- **Cubes**

  Write on the board: 19, 29, 39, 49, 59. Place the children in pairs. Say a 2-digit number with more than five units, e.g. 47. Each pair chooses a number from the board and adds it to 47.

  Point to each number in turn, asking for answers to the addition. Any pair with a correct answer takes a cube.

- **Number grid (1 to 100)**

  Point to a number on the grid, and say a number which is a near multiple of ten, e.g. 29. Everyone adds the two numbers mentally. After a few moments say: *Now!* The children shout out the answer. Does everyone agree?

  Repeat.

- Choose a child and say a 2-digit number. They add nine and say the answer. If correct that child chooses another and says a 2-digit number (boys should choose girls, girls should choose boys). The second child adds nine and says the answer. Continue around the class.

  Each child has three chances to make a mistake or hesitate.

5.4   Adding several numbers
Abacus 5   **Abacus 6**
N11   N11

- **Number cards (1 to 20)**

  Shuffle the cards and place them face down in a pile. Choose a child to take the top card and write the number on the board. They replace the card face down on the bottom of the pile. Choose another child to take a card. They read it aloud, then add it to the number on the board, writing the answer underneath. They replace the card on the bottom of the pile. Consult the class. Are they correct?

  Choose a child to take the next card and add it to the number on the board. Continue, keeping a running total.

  How large a total can the children make?

- **Two dice**

  Play 'Fish'. Divide the class into two teams. The teams take turns to throw both dice and add the numbers, writing the answer on the board. They continue throwing the dice and adding to the running total. If they throw a six the dice pass to the other team. If they throw a one, they lose their score for that round and pass on the dice. If they throw two ones, the other team shouts 'fish' and the first team lose their entire score.

  The first team to 50 wins.

5.5   Adding two or more 2-digit numbers

Abacus 5   **Abacus 6**
N11   N11

- Each child writes a 2-digit number on a piece of paper. Choose two children to each write their number on the board. They both add the numbers mentally and write the answer. Consult the class. Are they both correct?

  Repeat.

5.6   Adding 100 or multiples of 100

Abacus 5
N11

- **Cubes**

  Choose a child to write a 3-digit number on the board. Choose another child to add 100 and say the answer aloud. Choose another child to add 100 to this number and say the answer aloud. Continue until the total goes over 1000. The last child takes a cube.

  Start again with a different child writing the starting number.

- **A dice**

  Divide the class into two teams. Choose a child from Team A to write a 3-digit number on the board. Choose another child from Team A to throw the dice and write that number of hundreds on the board. Team A adds the two numbers and shouts the answer. Repeat for Team B.

  Which team's number is nearest to 500? They score a point.

  Play again.

5.7 Adding near multiples of 100

Abacus 5
N24

- Write on the board: 199, 499, 799, 599, 999, 299, 699, 99, 399, 899.

  Point to a number and ask the children to read it, e.g. *one hundred and ninety-nine*. Next ask them what this number is 'nearly'. They shout: *two hundred*.

  Continue for each number.

- Write 199 on the board. Choose a child and say a 3-digit number, e.g. 361 They add 199 and say the answer. If correct, that child chooses another and says a 3-digit number, e.g. 758. That child adds 199 and says the answer. Continue around the class.

  Each child has three chances to make a mistake or hesitate.

- **A dice**
  Divide the class into four teams and draw four columns on the board, one for each team. Each team chooses a 3-digit number and writes it in their column. Each team throws the dice and creates a number by multiplying by 100 and subtracting one, e.g. throw 3 make 299. They add to their first number and write the answer in their column. The team with an answer closest to 999 scores a point.

  Play again.

5.8 Adding two or more 3-digit numbers

Abacus 6

N11

- Write on the board: 349,
  529, 219, 789, 949, 669,
  179, 439.

  Choose a child to point to
  one number, e.g. 789. The
  class reads the number
  aloud.

  Choose another child to
  point to a second number,
  e.g. 219. Read that in
  unison. Each child should
  add the two numbers
  mentally. Take some
  answers and write them
  on the board.

  Complete the addition, by first rounding 789 to 790, then rounding
  219 to 220. Add these (discuss the different methods: 700 + 200 + 90 +
  20, or 790 + 200 + 20, or 800 + 220 – 10). Subtract 2 from the total to
  give the correct answer.

  Repeat.

5.9 Adding 1000

Abacus 5

N12

- Write a 4-digit number on the board. Read it in unison. Discuss which
  is the thousands digit, which is the hundreds, which is the tens and
  which is the units. Choose a child to add 1000 and write the answer
  underneath. Choose a child to add another 1000 and write the
  answer. Continue choosing children to add 1000 to the total (choose
  a confident child for 9925 + 1000 = 10 925).

  After ten or so children, start again with a new number.

5.10 Adding multiples of 1000

Abacus 5
N12

- **A dice**

    Write a 4-digit number on the board, e.g. 7392. Choose a child to throw the dice and write that number of thousands on the board. They add the two number and say the answer aloud. The class check they are correct. If so, that child chooses another and says a new 4-digit number. The second child writes it on the board, and throws the dice to find what must be added.

    Continue around the class, boys choosing girls, and girls choosing boys.

- **A dice**

    Write several 4-digit numbers on the board. Throw the dice. Each child chooses a number from the board, and adds the dice number of thousands to it. Ask several children for their answers. Which numbers did they choose?

    Repeat.

5.11 Adding near multiples of 1000

Abacus 5
N12, N24

- Write on the board: 1999, 4999, 9999, 2999, 999, 3999.

    Point to a number and ask the children to read it, e.g. *one thousand, nine hundred and ninety-nine*. Next ask them what this number is 'nearly'. They shout: *two thousand*.

    Continue for each number.

- **A dice**

    Write on the board: 999, 1999, 2999, 3999, 4999. Divide the class into four teams. Each team throws the dice four times to create a 4-digit number, e.g. 4241. Point to a number on the board. Each team must add the two numbers and write the answer on the board. The team with an answer closest to 7000 scores a point. Repeat

5.12 Adding whole numbers and decimals

Abacus 5
N38

Abacus 6
N10, N11, N24

- **A dice**
  Write on the board: 1·6, 3·2, 5·7, 4·8, 2·9. Choose a child to throw the dice and say the number aloud. They choose a number from the board without telling the class which number they are choosing. They add the two numbers and say the answer. The class guess which number they chose.

- Write a starting number on the board, e.g. 3·4. Choose a child and give them a whole number to add, e.g. 5. They must say the answer, i.e. *eight point four*. If correct, that child chooses another and gives them a whole number to add. Continue for four or five children, then start again with a different number.

5.13 Adding to the next tenth or the next whole number

Abacus 5
N38

Abacus 6
N10

- Choose a child and say a decimal number with tenths, e.g. 3·7. Ask them what is the next whole number and what must be added to make it. Write the addition on the board: 3·7 + 0·3 = 4·0. That child chooses another and says a decimal number with tenths. The second child says the next whole number and what must be added to make it. Continue around the class.

- **Number cards (0 to 10)**
  Place the children in pairs. Each pair writes three decimal numbers with tenths.

  Shuffle the cards and take the top one. Read the number and write it on the board, e.g. 7. Any pair who can add that many tenths to one of their numbers to make the next whole number can cross out that number. So if a pair has 4·3, they can cross it out. They can only cross out one number in each round.

  Continue until one pair has crossed out all their numbers: *Bingo!*

  Check their sheet against the numbers on the board.

  Variation Repeat for numbers with tenths and hundredths, adding to make the next tenth.

5.14 Adding two decimal numbers

Abacus 5
N36, N39

Abacus 6
N24

- Place the children in pairs. Each pair writes a decimal number with tenths. Choose two pairs to write their numbers on the board. Everyone adds the two numbers mentally. Ask the first two pairs to say their answer. Check with the class. Each pair scores a point for a correct answer.

  Repeat.

- **A dice**

  Write on the board: 1·9, 2·9, 3·9, 4·9, 5·9. Divide the class into four teams. Each team throws the dice twice and creates a decimal number with tenths. Each team chooses a number from the board to add. Ask for their answers and discuss what method they used (e.g. add 3 and take 0·1 off). The team with an answer closest to 10 scores a point.

  Play again.

5.15 Adding negative and positive numbers

Abacus 6
N29

- Draw a lift on the board. Label the ground zero, and floors above ground 1, 2, 3, ...; floors below ground ⁻1, ⁻2, ⁻3, ...

  Choose a child and say a starting floor. Ask them where they will be if they go up five floors. If correct, that child chooses another to give a floor and a number to add. Continue around the class.

- **Cubes, a dice (0 to 9)**

  Draw two columns on the board, one headed 'get' and one headed 'owe'. Divide the class into two teams: a 'gets' team and an 'owes' team. Each team throws the dice and writes the number in their column (with a '+' for the gets team and a '–' for the owes team). Consult the class: *I get £3 and owe £5. How much do I have? I owe £2.* Award the 'owes' team a point and give them a cube.

  Continue until one team has ten cubes.

Section 6: Subtraction

6.1 Subtracting a 1-digit number from a 2-digit number

Abacus 5
N25, N27

Abacus 6
N12

- Write a list of 2-digit numbers on the board, e.g. 32, 17, 47, 12, 84, 27, 15, 77.

  The children each take away 9 from each number, writing the answers on a sheet of paper. Remind them to add 10 and subtract 1. When they have finished they should stand up.

  When everyone is standing they should swap sheets with a partner, and mark the answers as you go through them on the board. Stress the adding 10 strategy throughout.

- Write on the board: 11, 17, 19, 14, 12, 16, 15, 18, 13. Divide the children into groups of three, and give each group a 1-digit number between 2 and 9. Some groups can have the same number.

  Each group then works against the clock to subtract their number from each number on the board.

  When the time is up ask each group in turn (i.e. starting with 2, then 3, 4, ... 9), to write their answers on the board underneath the original numbers. The class checks each group's work.

6.2 Subtracting 10 or multiples of 10

Abacus 5
N24, N27

- Choose a child and say a 2- or 3-digit number, e.g. 78. They subtract ten and say the answer, i.e. 68. If correct, that child chooses another and says a number. The second child subtracts ten and says the answer. Continue around the class, boys choosing girls and girls choosing boys.

  Each child has three chances to make a mistake or hesitate.

- Write a starting number on the board, e.g. 275. Choose a child to write the number ten less, i.e. 265. Choose another child to write the number ten less again, i.e. 255. Continue for each child. Chant down the list of numbers in unison.

Repeat with a different starting number.

Variation Subtract 20, 30 or 50.

- **A dice**
  Write on the board: 236, 92, 825, 81, 721, 77, 111.

  Divide the class into two teams. Choose a child to throw the dice and then subtract that many of tens from one of the numbers on the board (without saying which one). They should say the answer aloud. Their team must guess which number they chose. If correct, that team scores a point.

  Continue, choosing different children from each team, in turn.

6.3   Subtracting near multiples of 10

Abacus 5
N24, N27

Abacus 6
N11

- **Cubes**
  Write on the board: 19, 29, 39, 49, 59.

  Place the children in pairs. Choose a 2-digit starting number (with less than 5 units), e.g. 81. Each pair chooses a board number to take away from the starting number, and completes the subtraction. Point to each number in turn and ask any pair who subtracted this number for their answer. Do all the pairs agree? Any pair who is correct takes a cube.

- Choose a child and say a number. They subtract nineteen and say the answer. If correct, that child chooses another and says a new number. The second child subtracts nineteen and says the answer. Continue around the class, boys choosing girls and girls choosing boys.

  Each child has three chances to make a mistake or hesitate.

- Place the children in groups of three. Each group writes four 2-digit numbers larger than 50.

  Say a near multiple of ten, e.g. 49, and write it on the board. Each group chooses one of their numbers and subtracts your number, writing the answer. Repeat four times.

  Each group adds their four answers. The group closest to 50 wins.

6.4 Subtracting small numbers from large numbers

Abacus 5
N27

Abacus 6
N11, N12

- **Number grid (1 to 100)**

  Choose a child to point to a number on the grid that is larger than 30, e.g. 45. Choose another child and ask them to subtract six, and say the answer, i.e. 39. If correct the second child chooses a third to point to a new number and a fourth to subtract a 1-digit number.

  Encourage the children to partition when subtracting, i.e. 43 – 5 is best done as 43 – 3 then take away 2 more.

- **A dice, a timer**

  Write 100 on the board. Start the timer. The children take turns to throw the dice, subtract from the total on the board and write the new number. The dice then passes to the next child. How quickly can they reach zero?

6.5 Subtracting one 2-digit number from another

Abacus 5
N25, N27

Abacus 6
N12

- **Number grid (1 to 100)**

  Place the children in pairs. Each pair writes four 1-digit numbers on a piece of paper. Choose a child to close their eyes and point to the grid, e.g. 56. Write the number they point to, and subtract a number that is quite close, e.g. 56 – 48.

  The children complete the subtraction mentally. If the answer matches one of their numbers they can cross it out.

  Continue until one pair has crossed out all their numbers: *Bingo!*

6.6 Subtracting 100 or multiples of 100

Abacus 5
N24, N27

- Choose a child and say a 3-digit number, e.g. 797. They subtract one hundred and say the answer, i.e. 697. If correct, that child chooses another and says a number. The second child subtracts 100 and says the answer. Continue around the class, boys choosing girls and girls choosing boys.

  Each child has three chances to make a mistake or hesitate.

- Write a starting number on the board, e.g. 827. Choose a child to write the number 100 less, i.e. 727. Choose another child to write the number one hundred less again, i.e. 627. Continue until you reach a 2-digit number. Chant down the list in unison.

  Repeat with a different starting number.

  Variation Subtract 200.

- **A dice**
  Divide the class into two teams. Choose a child from Team A to write a 4-digit number on the board. Choose a child from Team B to throw the dice and write that number of hundreds, e.g. 300. Team B subtract the hundreds from the first number and write the answer. If they are correct they score a point.

  Play again swapping roles.

6.7 Subtracting near multiples of 100

Abacus 5
N24, N27

Abacus 6
N11

- **A dice**
  Place the children in pairs. Each pair writes a 4-digit number. Throw the dice, multiply it by 100 and subtract 1, e.g. throw 6, write 599.

  Each pair subtracts 599 from their number. Repeat five times, each time the children subtracting from their last answer.

  Any pair who reach zero stop playing. After the final round the pair with the smallest number wins.

- Choose a child and 'throw' them a 3-digit number. They subtract 99 and say the answer immediately. If correct, that child chooses another and says a 3-digit number. The second child subtracts 99 and says the answer. Continue around the class.

6.8 Subtracting small numbers from 3- or 4-digit numbers

Abacus 5
N25

Abacus 6
N12

- **Number cards (1 to 9)**
  Divide the children into groups of three. Each group writes a 3-digit number. Shuffle the cards and place them face down in a pile. Take the top card and call out the number, e.g. 7. Each group subtracts the card from their number and writes the answer. Continue for each card in the pile, the children subtracting each time from their last answer.

  At the end check each group's work (the difference between the starting number and the final answer should be 45).

  Groups which are correct score 10 points. Play again.

- **A dice, a timer**
  Write 1000 on the board. Start the timer. The children take turns to throw the dice, subtract from the total on the board and write the new number. The dice then passes to the next child. How quickly can they reach 900?

6.9 Subtracting whole numbers from decimal numbers

Abacus 5
N41

Abacus 6
N11, N26

- **A dice**

    Write a decimal number more than 6 on the board, e.g. 7·7. Choose a child to throw the dice. They subtract the number thrown from the board number and say the answer. If correct, that child chooses another and says a decimal number (more than 6) to be written on the board. The second child throws the dice and subtracts it from the board number. Continue around the class.

- Write 20·7 on the board. Choose a child to subtract 3 and write the answer. Choose another child to subtract 3 from the last number and write the answer. Continue until the answer reaches 2·7.

    Repeat with a different starting number, trying to keep up the pace.

6.10 Subtracting two decimal numbers

Abacus 5
N41

Abacus 6
N26

- Place the children in pairs. Each pair writes a decimal number (tenths) less than 20. Choose two pairs to write their numbers on the board, e.g. 5·7 and 8·4 The rest of the class subtract the smaller number from the larger. The first two pairs write their answers on the board. Check with the class. Discuss the strategy, e.g. 5·7 + 0·3 = 6; 6 + 2·4 = 8·4; so 2·4 + 0·3 = 2·7.

    Repeat.

- Write on the board: 1·9, 2·9, 3·9, 4·9, 5·9.

    Place the children in pairs. Each pair writes a decimal number (tenths) more than 7 on a piece of paper. Point to a number on the board, which the children subtract from their number. Ask pairs for their answers. The pair with an answer closest to 3 scores a point.

    Repeat.

Section 7: Multiplication

7.1 Doubling

Abacus 5
N5, N16

Abacus 6
N4, N6

- Choose a child and say a starting number, e.g. 3. They double it and say the answer. If correct, that child chooses another, who must double again. Continue around the class until you reach a 3-digit number.

  Start again with a different number.

- **A dice**
  Divide the class into two teams. Team A throw the dice twice to create a 2-digit number. They agree its double and write this down. Team B do the same. Both teams then write their doubles on the board. Teams score one point for a correct answer. Play again.

7.2 Trebling

Abacus 5
N6, N18, N19

Abacus 6
N6, N17

- Choose three children to stand facing away from the board. The first child thinks of a number between 1 and 30 with less than 6 units, e.g. 24. They write it on the board. The second child trebles the number and writes the answer on the board. The third child (facing away from the board) trebles the first number and says the answer aloud. Do the written and spoken numbers match?

  Repeat.

7.3 Multiplication facts

Abacus 5
N3, N5, N6, N16,
N17, N18, N19

Abacus 6
N3, N4, N6, N19

- Choose a child and give them a multiplication fact, e.g. 4×8. They should answer immediately. If they can, they choose another child and give them a multiplication fact. Continue around the class.

- Choose a child and give them a multiplication fact, e.g. 6 × 7, and an animal, e.g. a duck. That child answers the question in the voice of a duck! Choose another child and give them a different fact and a different animal.
- Draw this table on the board:

5	4	6	7	9	11
3					
5					
7					
8					
9					

Choose a child to write an answer in the table. If they are correct, immediately select another child to write a different answer. Time the children. How quickly can they complete the table? Practise regularly.

- Divide the class into four teams: 'sixes', 'sevens', 'eights', 'nines'. Each team must write all its multiples on the board as quickly as possible. Each child in a team must write at least one multiple, and no one can write more than two.

7.4   Multiplying a 2-digit number by 10
Abacus 5
N15, N17

- **Number grid (1 to 100)**
  Choose a child and point to a number on the grid. They say that number aloud, multiply it by 10 and say the answer. Write both numbers on the board. If correct, that child can choose another and point to a number on the grid. Continue around the class.
- Address the whole class, saying ten 2-digit numbers in quick succession. The children multiply each by ten and write the answer. They can then swap papers and check each others answers. Write each number and answer on the board.

7.5   Multiplying a 2-digit number by 9

Abacus 5   **Abacus 6**
N3, N6, N19   N5, N17

- **Number grid (1 to 100)**
  Divide the class into two teams. Point to a number on the grid, e.g.
  43. Choose a child in Team A to multiply it by 10 and write the
  answer on the board, i.e. 430. Choose a child in the Team B to
  subtract the first number and write the answer, i.e. 387. Point out that
  this is the first number multiplied by 9.
  $43 \times 9 = 387$. Repeat, swapping roles.

- Show the children this trick. Write a 2-digit number multiplied by 9
  on the board, e.g. $68 \times 9 =$. Point out that the answer must be 3-
  digit. Explain that the first digit of the answer is usually the same as
  the tens digit of the first number, i.e. 6. Explain that the last digit of
  the answer usually makes ten with the units digit of the first number,
  i.e. 2. Remind the children that the digits of the final answer must
  add up to a multiple of 9. We already have 6 and 2, so the middle
  digit must be 1, i.e. $68 \times 9 = 612$. Check by multiplying 68 by 10 and
  subtracting 68.

  This trick often works, but sometimes doesn't. Place the children in
  pairs to investigate.

7.6   Multiplying a 2-digit number by 11 or 12

Abacus 5   **Abacus 6**
N6, N19   N5, N17

- Divide the class into groups of three. Each group writes a
  2-digit number more than 30, and multiplies it
  by 10. Then they double the first number and
  add it to the answer. Ask groups to write
  their numbers on the board, pointing
  out that this is the same as
  multiplying by 12.

  Repeat for multiplying
  by 11.

7.7 Multiplying by a multiple of 10

Abacus 5
N18

Abacus 6
N5

- Place the children in pairs. Choose a pair and say a 2-digit number, e.g. 36. Write it on the board. The pair multiply it by 20: one child doubles and the other multiplies by 10. They write the answer on the board. The rest of the class check.

  Continue for different pairs.

  Variation Multiply by 30, by first trebling the number and then multiplying by ten.

  Variation Multiply by 40 by doubling twice and then multiplying by ten.

7.8 Multiplying a 2-digit number by a near multiple of 10

Abacus 5
N6, N16

Abacus 6
N17, N31

- Divide the class into groups of three. Give each group a 2-digit number more than 20. Explain that they are going to multiply by 19. Write 19, and say in unison: *nineteen is nearly twenty*.

  In their groups one child doubles the number, the second multiplies the result by 10, and the third subtracts the original number.

  Each group writes their original number and answer on the board. Check with the class. Each team which is correct scores ten points.

  Repeat.

7.9 Approximating multiplication

Abacus 5
N30, N31, N32

Abacus 6
N18, N30, N32

- **Pencil and paper or calculators**
  Divide the class into groups of three. Write a multiplication for each group horizontally on the board, e.g. 24×38, 33×37, 28×43, 36×42. Each group finds an approximate answer to their multiplication and quickly writes the approximation on the board. So, for 24×38, that group might find 20×40 and write 800.

  The groups check on paper or with a calculator. Who was closest?

  Play again.

- **Number cards (2 to 10)**
  Shuffle the cards and place them face down in a pile. Divide the class into teams of approximately eight. Each team writes three multiples of 100 on the board, e.g. 300, 600, 700. Write a starting number on the board, e.g. 82.

  Take a number card, e.g. 5. Each team works together to approximate 5 × 82, i.e. 400. Any team with 400 as a multiple can cross it out.

  Repeat for a new card. After several cards change the target number.

  The first team to cross out all three numbers wins.

7.10 Multiplying by 100

Abacus 5
N15

Abacus 6
N15

- Choose a child and say a 2- or 3-digit number. They multiply by 100 and say the answer. Choose another child to write the answer on the board. Is it correct? If so, the first child chooses another and says a 2- or 3-digit number to be multiplied by 100.

  Continue around the class.

- Write a multiplication on the board, e.g. 300 × 100. Write four possible answers, e.g. 300, 3000, 30 000, 300 000. The children each write down the one they think is correct on a piece of paper. Point to each answer, taking votes for each one. Discuss which is correct and why.

  Repeat for a different multiplication and different answers.

7.11 Multiplying by multiples of 100

Abacus 5
N18

Abacus 6
N5

- **Two sets of number cards (1 to 9)**
  Place the children in pairs. Each pair writes four different numbers (each a multiple of 1000, and less than 20 000), e.g. 13 000, 19 000, 11 000, 16 000.

  Shuffle the cards and place them face down in a pile. Take two cards and read them out. Each pair uses the cards to make a 2-digit number and multiplies it by 200 (by first doubling, then multiplying by 100). Check each pair's answer.

Round each answer to the nearest 1000. Any pair with a rounded number on their sheet can cross it out.

Continue until one pair has crossed out all their numbers.

7.12 Multiplying decimals by 10

Abacus 6
N15

- Choose a child and 'throw' a decimal number (tenths) at them. Write it on the board. They multiply it by ten and say the answer immediately. Write it on the board. Consult the class. Is it correct? If so, that child chooses another and says a decimal number (tenths). The second child multiplies by ten and says the answer.

  Continue around the class.

- Write five decimal numbers (tenths) on the board, e.g. 1·7, 3·3, 4·1, 9·2, 8·4. Choose five children, one for each number. They each multiply their number by ten and write the answer on the board. The rest of the class check their answers. Each child who is correct scores a point.

  Repeat with different numbers and children.

7.13 Multiplying decimals by 100

Abacus 6
N15

- Place the children in pairs. Each pair writes down a decimal number (tenths), e.g. 5·2. Encourage the more able children to write a number more than ten. Ask each pair to multiply their number by 100. Choose 6 pairs to write their numbers and answers on the board. Check each pair's numbers. Are they correct?

  Choose another six children and repeat.

Section 8: Division

8.1 Division facts

Abacus 5
N3, N5, N6, N20

Abacus 6
N3, N4, N19

- Write a 1-digit number on the board, e.g. 4. Choose a child and as: *How many fours in thirty-two?* They should reply immediately. If correct, that child chooses another and asks them a fours fact, e.g. *How many fours in twenty-eight?*

  Continue around the class.

- Draw a division table on the board.

÷	32	48	56	24	64
8					

Divide the class into teams of five. Start with Team A. Ask a child to write one of the answers in a space. Choose a second child from the same team to fill in another space. Continue until the table is filled in. How many did Team A get correct? Keep score.

Change the numbers for Team B.

÷	45	27	54	72	63
9					

Repeat for each team in turn. Encourage the class to help each team as they fill in their table.

- **8 dice**

  Divide the class into teams of approximately four. Write 2, 3, 4, 5, 6, 9, 10 along the top of the board, circling each one.

  Each team throws their dice three times to make a 3-digit number, which they write on the board.

  Together each team finds which circled numbers divide into their number, using the tests for divisibility.

  Check each team's answers. They score 1 point for each correct answer. If none of the circle numbers divide into their number, they score 6 points.

  Repeat.

8.2　Halving

Abacus 5
N5, N16, N17, N20

Abacus 6
N4, N6

- Write on the board: 10, 20, 30, 40, 50, 60, 70, 80, 90, 100, 110, 120. Place the children in teams of five or six. Each group has three minutes (time them) to halve each number.

  After three minutes ask one member from each team to write their answers on the board.

  Compare the team's answers. Each team scores one point for a correct answer.

  Play again with a different set of numbers, e.g. 16, 32, 48, 64, 96, 112, 128, 144.

- Choose a child and 'throw' them an even number, e.g. 26. They halve it and say the answer immediately, i.e. *thirteen*. If correct, that child chooses another and gives them a number to halve. If they are incorrect give them another number to halve.

  Continue rapidly around the class.

8.3　Remainders

Abacus 5
N4, N9, N33, N34

Abacus 6
N20, N33

- **Number grid (1 to 100), a dice**
  Place the children in pairs. Each pair writes five 1-digit numbers on a piece of paper. Point at an odd 2-digit number on the grid and throw the dice. In pairs, the children divide the grid number by the dice number. Check with several pairs what their answers are, and write the division on the board, e.g. 35 ÷ 2 = 17 r 1. Any pair with a number that matches the remainder may cross it out. If you throw a 1, count this as a remainder of 7.

  Continue until one pair has crossed out all their numbers: *Bingo!*

8.4 Dividing by 10

Abacus 5
N15

Abacus 6
N2, N16

- Write on the board: 350, 460, 120, 770, 110, 410, 930, 550.

  Choose a child to choose one of these numbers, divide it by ten and say the answer aloud. The rest of the class says which number they originally chose. Write the answer next to the number. Choose another child and repeat.

  Continue until each number has been divided by 10.

  Repeat for more difficult numbers, e.g. 1100, 23 030, 4470, 2020, 5550, 10 100, 4560, 20 000, 4070.

- Write on the board: 9 900 000. Read the number in unison: *Nine million, nine hundred thousand. How many times can this number be divided by ten?*

  Choose a child to divide it by 10 and say the answer. Write it on the board. Consult the class. Are they correct?

  Choose another child to divide the first answer by 10 and say the result. Write the answer on the board.

  Continue until the answer reaches 99.

8.5 Dividing by 100

Abacus 6
N2, N16

- Write a multiple of 100 on the board, e.g. 3500. Choose a child and ask them to read the number aloud. Consult the class. Are they correct? If so, that child chooses another who must divide the first number by 100 and say the answer, i.e. 35. Write it on the board. Consult the class. Are they correct? If so, the second child chooses another.

  Write a different number on the board, e.g. 10 100. The third child reads it aloud, and, if correct, chooses another to divide by 100.

  Continue around the class.

8.6 Approximating division

Abacus 5
N33, N34

Abacus 6
N30, N33, N34

- **Pencil and paper or calculators**

Place the children in groups of four. Write divisions on the board, one for each group: $377 \div 6$, $269 \div 5$, $199 \div 4$, $318 \div 4$, $562 \div 3$, $419 \div 5$, $231 \div 4$, $297 \div 6$.

Each group agrees an approximate answer to their division (only give them one minute). One child from each group writes their approximate answer on the board, and explains how they made the approximation. Award points for good methods.

Each group then uses pencil and paper or a calculator to complete the division. Write the correct answers on the board. How close were the approximations? Award points for those that are close.

Repeat.

- **A dice**

Divide the class into teams of approximately eight. Each team writes three numbers between 40 and 100 on the board, e.g. 57, 89, 91. Write a target number on the board, e.g. 10 (a multiple of 5 between 10 and 50).

Each team throws the dice and chooses a number to divide. They find an approximate answer, and if it matches the target, they cross that number from their list. The teams should check each other's approximations.

Write a new target number and repeat.

The first team to cross out all their numbers wins.

Section 9: Algebra

9.1 Solving simple equations

Abacus 6
N42, M4, M5

- Write $52 + m = 94$ on the board. Choose a child to say what m is. Write down their suggestion. Consult the class. Are they correct?

  Place the children in pairs. Each pair must make up an equation and write it down. They record the solution on a separate piece of paper. Each pair swaps equations with another pair, and tries to solve the mystery. Each pair then checks the other's work.

  Go around the class awarding points to each pair who correctly solved the equation.

  Repeat.

Section 10: Shape

10.1 2-d shape

Abacus 5
S1, S2, S3

Abacus 6
S7, S8, S9

- Write the name of a shape on the board, e.g. pentagon. Each child has three minutes to draw an unusually-shaped pentagon (without using rulers). After three minutes they compare shapes, checking they are pentagons. Choose several children to draw their shapes on the board, Discuss each one. Does anyone else have a similar shape?

  Repeat for a different shape, e.g. hexagon.

- Ask the children to draw a shape, giving them explicit instructions, e.g. *Draw a hexagon with three or more right angles.* After several minutes ask different children to draw their shape on the board. Check that the class agree it matches the instruction. Can anyone draw a hexagon with four right-angles? With five?

  Repeat for other instructions, e.g. *Draw a pentagon with at least two angles which are less than 90°; Draw a quadrilateral with two angles which are more than 90°; Draw a pentagon with three right angles; Draw an octagon with 4 angles less than 90°.*

10.2 3-d shape

Abacus 5
S5

Abacus 6
S6

- Describe a 3-d shape to the children, e.g. *It has two flat faces and one curved face. It has two edges and no corners. It will roll. What shape is it?* They shut heir eyes and imagine the shape. Can anyone name it?

  Repeat, e.g. *It has four flat faces, and no curved sides. It has four corners. It has six edges.* When the children are confident ask a child to describe a shape for the others to guess.

10.3 Angles

Abacus 5
S8, S9, S10

Abacus 6
S1, S2

- Divide the class into three teams: 'acute', 'obtuse', 'reflex'. Each team must look around the class, trying to find one example of their type of angle. Can they find more than one? After a few minutes ask if each team has found an angle. Discuss each one, then as a class look for others (clock hands, door making an angle with the wall, books, cards, desks, ...).

- Divide the class into groups of four. Each group draws a clock, and marks a time on it. They calculate the approximate size of the angle between the hands. Choose a group to read out their angle. Can the other groups guess what the corresponding time might be? Let them have several guesses, asking the team to give clues.

Repeat for each group in turn.

10.4 Triangles

Abacus 5
S3

Abacus 6
S2

- **Protractors**

  Describe a triangle to the children, for them to draw, e.g. *Draw a triangle which has an angle of about 45° and another angle of about 60°.* They should try to draw the triangle without a protractor. The children compare results and can check the angles using a protractor.

  Repeat for other triangles, e.g. *Draw a triangle where one angle is more than 150°; Draw a triangle where all three angles are the same.*

  When the children are confident, they can take turns to describe a triangle for the others to draw.

- Give each child a piece of paper to fold in half. Next they tear or cut off a corner at the fold to make a triangle. Ask them to make an equilateral triangle, or a right-angled triangle. Ask them to make an obtuse-angled triangle, and acute-angled triangle. Can they make a triangle which is not isosceles?

10.5 Coordinates

Abacus 5
S7

Abacus 6
S3

- Each child draws a coordinate grid on squared paper from ⁻10 to 10. Each child decides where on the grid to place some treasure, without telling anyone else. They should mark the treasure on their grid. Read out pairs of coordinates for the children to mark on their grids. Each time a child's treasure is found, they are 'out'. The last child remaining is the winner.

Section 11: Measurement

11.1 Metric units

Abacus 5
M1, M2, M5

Abacus 6
M1, M2, M3

- Write on the board: 100 cm = 1 m, 1000 mm = 1 m, 1000 m = 1 km.

  Choose a child and say a length, e.g. 50 cm, writing it on the board. They must say the same measurement in another unit, e.g. 500 mm. They write it on the board. Ask for other suggestions from the class, e.g. 0·5 m. If correct, that child chooses another and says a length for them to convert.

  Continue around the class.

  Variation Repeat for weight (kilograms and grams), or capacity (litres and millilitres).

- Write on the board: length, weight, capacity, time, temperature.

  Say a unit, e.g. litres. Each child writes what dimension that unit measures, i.e. capacity. Discuss what you might measure with that unit, e.g. shampoo, petrol, lemonade.

  Repeat for different units.

- Write on the board: millimetres, centimetres, metres, kilometres.

  Choose a child and say an object, e.g. beetle. Which units would they use to measure it? They may have to justify their answer (e.g. it could possibly be centimetres, though it is more likely millimetres). Check that the class agree. If so , that child chooses another and says an object.

Continue around the class. Discuss the answers. Some objects may have more than one answer.

11.2 Time

Abacus 5
M6, M7

- Run through some time questions at a good pace. Ask the children to write the answers.

  How many days in a week?

  How many days in a year?

  How many days in September?

  How many months in a year?

  How many months in two years?

  How many years in a century?

  How many days in February?

  How many hours in a day?

  How many hours in a week?

  How many weeks in a year?

  Ask them to make a sensible estimate if they are not sure. Go through each answer, discussing each one. Focus on key facts: 24 hours in a day. Seven days in a week. Twelve months in a year, ...

- Place the children in small groups to work on some time problems: *How many days have we been at school in all? How many months are there till the turn of the century? How many years is one million days?* Discuss ways of solving the problems.

- Choose a child and say a time in 24 hour clock, e.g. *eighteen hundred.* They say the time in 12 hour clock, i.e. *six o'clock in the evening* (or *six p.m.*). Continue around the class, giving some more difficult times, e.g. *fourteen thirty.*

- Use a timetable with times in 24 hour clock. Read out a time and write it on the board, e.g. *The train arrives at 15:02.* The class shout back: *The train arrives at two minutes past three.* Ensure they repeat the answer in unison.